The Great PenGuin ReScue

Saving the African Penguins

Sandra Markle

M Millbrook Press • Minneapolis

For Scott Fillner and the children of Bowman Woods
Elementary School in Cedar Rapids, Iowa

Acknowledgments: The author would like to thank the following people for sharing their enthusiasm and expertise: Peter Barham, professor, University of Bristol, United Kingdom; Romy Klusener, Chick Rearing Unit supervisor at SANCCOB; Nola Parsons, veterinarian at SANCCOB; Christoph Schwitzer, Director of Conservation, Bristol Zoological Society; Heather Urquhart, senior aquarist, New England Aquarium; and Stephen van der Spuy, executive director, SANCCOB. A special thank-you to Skip Jeffery for his loving support during the creative process.

Text copyright © 2018 by Sandra Markle

Millbrook Press
A division of Lerner Publishing Group, Inc.
241 First Avenue North
Minneapolis, MN 55401 USA

For reading levels and more information, look up this title at www.lernerbooks.com.

Main body text set in Metro Office 12/18. Typeface provided by Linotype AG.

Library of Congress Cataloging-in-Publication Data

Names: Markle, Sandra, author.
Title: The great penguin rescue : saving the African penguins / by Sandra Markle.
Description: Minneapolis : Millbrook Press, [2017] | Audience: Ages 9–12. | Audience: Grades 4 to 6. | Includes bibliographical references and index.
Identifiers: LCCN 2016042675 (print) | LCCN 2016053518 (ebook) | ISBN 9781512413151 (lb : alk. paper) | ISBN 9781512451122 (eb pdf)
Subjects: LCSH: African penguin—Conservation—South Africa—Juvenile literature. | Animal rescue—South Africa—Juvenile literature. | Oil spills and wildlife—South Africa—Juvenile literature. | Sea birds—Conservation—South Africa—Juvenile literature.
Classification: LCC QL696.S473 M3578 2017 (print) | LCC QL696.S473 (ebook) | DDC 598.47—dc23

LC record available at https://lccn.loc.gov/2016042675

Manufactured in the United States of America
1-39774-21312-1/30/2017

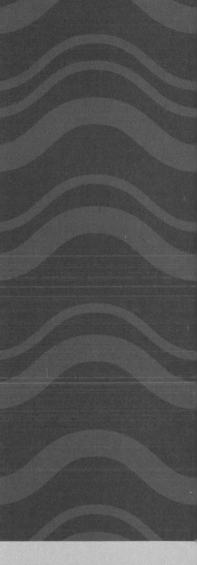

TABLE OF CONTENTS

Even though this penguin still has her downy chick coat, she's already nearly adult height.

On a mild June evening, a three-month-old female African penguin chick wiggles out of her family's nest under a tree. She straightens up tall and moans in short bursts, over and over. It's the way a penguin chick says, *I'm hungry. Please feed me.*

Her nesting colony in South Africa is full of activity at this time of year, full of breeding pairs raising chicks. And each evening, the adults come ashore after feeding all day in the South Atlantic Ocean. When this little female's parents return from the ocean with food in their bellies, they'll find her and bring up partly digested fish from their stomachs for her to eat. But they're not back yet, so she sits outside the nest and waits.

Adult African penguins spend most of their time in the water, except when they come ashore to nest and raise chicks or to molt (shed and replace their feathers).

Shadows knit together. Other chicks are nearby, waiting by their nests too. At last, donkey-like brays fill the air as the adult African penguins return from the ocean.

With feathered coats still shiny and wet from the surf, the adults waddle ashore on Robben Island, off the coast of Cape Town. Parents will feed their chicks and huddle with them in their nest overnight. Then, in the morning, the adults will head back to the ocean to catch more fish— another day's meal for themselves and their chicks.

The young female chick moans and peeps as adults pass by. A few adults pause and bray at her. None claim her.

Check out the bristly inside of the penguin's mouth. Its tongue has toothlike barbs that help push food down its throat.

Look closely and you'll see a few bits of twigs under the chick. Penguin parents collect twigs and grasses to build their nests.

The female chick waits for her parents until the path from the beach is empty. Then she wiggles back inside her family's nest. Snug inside, she listens to the night sounds and sleeps.

Sometimes parents have to travel farther than usual to find enough to eat, and they spend the night on the ocean. But that night and another day passes, and the little female is still waiting for her parents to come back and feed her.

When they're not hunting, nesting penguins guard their chicks in the nest. Their scaly feet give off body heat so the birds don't get too warm in the sunshine.

African penguin chicks need to eat nearly every day to grow up strong enough to swim and catch fish for themselves. So when a second day and night passes without any food, the female chick is very hungry. By the third evening, when her parents still don't return, she wanders away from the nest, peeping and moaning, begging to be fed.

At three months old, the female chick is close to fledging, when she'll shed her fluffy down coat and grow feathers. Until she does, though, she can't swim and catch fish for herself. She's on her own and needs help—or she won't survive.

PENGUINS IN TROUBLE

Unfortunately, that young female isn't unusual. The entire African penguin population is in danger, having reached critically low numbers. In the early 1800s, scientists estimate, there were around four million African penguins. By 2014 BirdLife South Africa, a conservation organization, estimated that only about twenty-four thousand breeding pairs remained.

Experts debate the total number of adult African penguins. But all agree the population is at risk of becoming extinct in the wild.

What happened that left these birds with a tiny fraction of their original numbers?

Much of the decline has come from humans interfering with the penguins' nesting sites. African penguins come ashore to lay their eggs and raise chicks. And they mainly come ashore at twenty-seven sites along the southwestern part of Africa, in the countries of South Africa and Namibia.

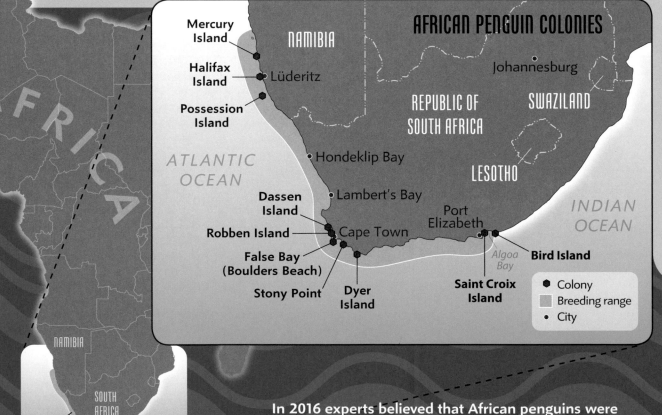

In 2016 experts believed that African penguins were breeding and nesting at about twenty-seven colonies in South Africa and Namibia. The colonies shown here are the largest and are key to the penguins' survival.

Many penguins at the Dassen Island colony nest in dug-out areas of ground.

Where the penguins raise their young, they form groups called colonies. This may be as few as fifty breeding pairs or as many as thousands. Being part of a colony means an adult can easily find a mate or reconnect with its mate from other years. African penguins may keep the same mate for several years or even for life.

Over time, though, human activities have hurt the penguin colonies. First, people changed the nesting sites by removing the guano—bird poop—from the surface.

For centuries, African penguins, gulls, and other seabirds came to the same breeding sites year after year. So the surface soil at those sites was topped with a thick layer of guano. While that may not sound appealing, the piled-up guano was just what the penguins needed. A penguin could use its claw-tipped toes to scratch out a burrow to shelter its nest. The guano above the dug-out space remained hard, so the burrow roof didn't cave in. And the guano insulated the burrow from the hot sun during the day. On cool nights, it retained just enough heat to keep the nest warm.

But people discovered the guano could help them too. Before artificial fertilizer was invented, animal waste was the best fertilizer to help crops grow. Fertilizer adds nutrients to the soil, which helps plants grow healthy and strong. So beginning in the mid-nineteenth century, people dug up the guano from breeding sites and sold it to farmers. Once machines were able to do this job, the guano was removed even faster. Eventually the nesting sites were scraped bare. What was left was mostly sand, and when the penguins dug burrows, the roofs quickly crumbled.

At most nesting sites, temperatures are mild. February and March are some of the warmest months, with highs near 80°F (27°C). But nests without shade can get too warm in the sun.

African penguins have been forced to nest in the open at many sites, including here at Boulders Beach in Cape Town.

At some sites, penguin parents are still able to nest in the shelter of large rocks or plants. At others, African penguins are forced to nest in the open. Then the parents may get too warm, needing to abandon their eggs and chicks while they dive into the ocean to cool off. That leaves the nests unprotected from predators such as kelp gulls.

Open nests offer even less security as the African penguin population dwindles. In the past, nests crowded together in a colony would have offered group protection for the eggs and chicks from predators. But in recent years, because there are fewer penguins, the nests are spread out, even in larger colonies. So there's less protection for the chicks.

Guano isn't the only thing people have taken from the penguin nesting sites. Until the late 1960s, people also collected the African penguins' eggs.

The guano diggers were the first to eat penguin eggs, which are a little larger than chicken eggs. Soon penguin eggs were considered a treat because they were said to taste pleasantly fishy, and in the early 1900s, restaurants throughout South Africa were serving them. African penguin eggs were also shipped to restaurants in other countries. Collecting and selling penguin eggs became big business.

A basket of penguin eggs, collected on Dassen Island, would have been in high demand in the early 1900s. During the breeding season, even the South African Parliament ate penguin eggs at a weekly breakfast.

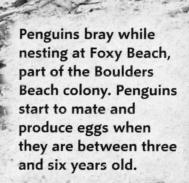

Penguins bray while nesting at Foxy Beach, part of the Boulders Beach colony. Penguins start to mate and produce eggs when they are between three and six years old.

Scientists estimate that from 1900 through the 1930s, at least half of all the African penguin eggs laid were collected each year. Most people didn't imagine this could cause a problem. They believed that African penguins, like chickens, would endlessly produce more eggs. But African penguins produce only two eggs each breeding season. And most breed just once a year, although some breed twice a year. The breeding rate wasn't enough to keep the population from shrinking drastically as eggs were removed from the colonies.

By the mid-1900s, the demand for penguin eggs had dwindled as people became aware of the impact on the birds. Finally, in 1967, the South African government passed a law that banned collecting African penguin eggs. Some people, however, continued to collect eggs illegally.

Unfortunately, the trouble for these penguins wasn't over yet. Even as the population decreased, the threats to their survival increased.

FROM BAD TO WORSE

Twentieth-century technology and environmental changes brought fresh challenges for African penguins.

First, the penguins faced steeper competition for their food. In 1935 commercial fishing fleets began to replace individual boats harvesting fish off the South African coast. The industry boomed during World War II (1939–1945), with a new demand for canned fish. By then ships had better engines and could travel farther to catch fish.

After the war, the commercial fishing fleet also had a new technology called sonar (a device using sound waves bounced off objects) to locate schools of fish. And as the number of ships harvesting fish increased, so did the size of the catch. Commercial boats caught small fish such as sardines and anchovies. Those same fish are the main food for African penguins. The result was a lot more fish for people—and a lot less for African penguin parents to catch and share with their chicks.

A purse seine net is dropped down and pulled shut like a drawstring purse to capture a large part or even an entire school of fish.

The Penguin Cycle

Adult African penguins usually breed and nest from February through September. The parents take turns sitting on the eggs, keeping them in contact with their brood patch (an area of bare skin). This keeps the eggs just the right temperature while the chicks inside develop. After about forty days, the chicks hatch. Then, for the next month, the parents take turns swimming off to fish and staying to guard and feed the chicks. After that, both parents spend every day in the ocean, feeding on fish. And they return each evening to feed the chicks and huddle with them, keeping them safe and warm as the temperature drops overnight.

A few days after mating, the female African penguin lays her first egg. About two days later, she lays one more.

By the time the chicks are four months old, they have grown their juvenile (young adult) feathers, and the parents leave them. The chicks get hungry without food and follow the adults into the ocean. There they quickly begin to swim and catch fish.

However, with the daily threats of predators, less than 25 percent of the young that leave the colony survive to become breeding adults. African penguins usually don't breed until they are between three and six years old. And as many as 20 percent of adults either never breed or only breed occasionally. So of all the juveniles leaving the breeding colony, only a few return to begin the life cycle over again.

Young adults, such as the penguin on the left, have slate blue rather than black backs. This changes to black when they molt as adults, at two or three years old.

Over time, the penguins also had to swim farther to find their food. African penguins hunt in areas near an upwelling, a current of deep ocean water that rises to the surface. This upwelling brings nutrients to sunlit areas near the surface. The nutrients help tiny ocean-living plants to grow. Then tiny animals feed on these plants at the upwelling sites, and in turn, they are food for little fish, such as sardines and anchovies, the penguins' main food.

Along southwestern Africa, coastal winds push surface waters offshore, and the Benguela upwelling brings up nutrients as it replaces the coastal water. This area has long been a rich feeding ground for penguins. However, since the late 1800s, Earth's average air and water temperatures have been warming. In 2004 scientists realized this climate change had shifted the South African coastal winds and the Benguela upwelling farther offshore—farther from the penguin colonies.

Surface winds push surface water away from an area.

Warmer surface water moves offshore.

phytoplankton and zooplankton (microscopic)

small fish

Deeper, colder, nutrient-rich water rises up from beneath the surface to replace the water that was pushed away.

nutrients

UPWELLING

An adult African penguin usually only has the time and energy to swim about 12 miles (19 kilometers) away from its colony and back in a day while catching fish.

As a result, penguin parents have had to travel farther to reach their supply of fish. That means they spend more energy traveling and take longer to return to their hungry chicks. And they may still return without full bellies.

When penguin parents don't have as much fish to feed their chicks, the chicks develop more slowly. Slow growth is a life-threatening problem, because by the time the chicks are about four months old—whether or not they're ready to be on their own—the parents must abandon them. The adults have to prepare to molt, shedding all their old feathers and growing new ones. So chicks that have been underfed and aren't ready to find their own food will struggle to survive.

Penguin's New Clothes

An African penguin's feathers are like its clothes. They overlap to form a thick covering, with an outer waterproof part that keeps the bird's skin dry. The downy inner part of the feathers helps insulate the penguin, shielding its skin from the cold ocean water and from the hot sun while it's nesting. Over time, some feathers become badly worn or broken. So each year, a penguin sheds its entire coat at one time and grows a new one. This molt usually happens sometime between September and January—spring and summer in Earth's Southern Hemisphere.

It takes a penguin about three weeks to a month to replace all its feathers, including preening time at the end to waterproof its new coat. And to get ready to molt, a penguin needs to eat a lot for a few weeks. That helps its body develop new feathers. It also builds up body fat. While molting, a penguin can't hunt, because it lacks its protective coat and has to stay ashore. So it burns the extra body fat for energy.

That's why African penguin parents are on a strict timeline for leaving their young. An adult simply can't catch fish for its chicks while it's getting ready to molt or during its molt.

Penguins have more feathers than most birds—as many as 100 per square inch (6.4 square centimeters). African penguins shed their feathers in fluffy patches *(right)* as they molt.

African penguin numbers were still falling in the 1970s, after guano harvesting and egg collecting had ended. To help save the penguins, the government passed laws in the late 1980s to protect the penguin colony sites as nature preserves. But that still didn't slow the population decline.

Even as people were discussing other actions to try to help African penguins, catastrophe struck.

On June 23, 2000, a bulk ore carrier called the *MV Treasure* developed a hole in its hull and sank 6 miles (9.6 km) off the coast of South Africa, leaking fuel oil. This oil spill was South Africa's worst environmental disaster in history. The ship was carrying a full load of fuel, dumping oil between Dassen Island and Robben Island—the first- and third-largest African penguin colonies—during the breeding season. The spill oiled thousands of adults that were fishing at sea.

On Robben Island, volunteers round up oiled penguins for transport to the emergency cleaning center.

When oil coats a bird, its feathers stick together in clumps, exposing its skin to the irritating oil and to cold ocean water. So the bird begins to preen (run its feathers through its beak to clean and straighten them). But it swallows oil in the process, which harms its digestive system. Meanwhile, bobbing on the oil-coated ocean, the bird also breathes in fumes that hurt its lungs. All of this damage can kill the adult. Then its chicks aren't fed, and they die too.

The oil spill was such a serious threat to the African penguins that the International Bird Rescue Research Center (IBRRC) launched an effort to save the penguins—and other kinds of oiled seabirds—the same day the accident happened.

Volunteers use a toothbrush to gently clean the bird's head.

Rescuers usually use Dawn liquid soap to clean an oiled bird because it removes the oil without irritating the bird's skin or eyes.

The *MV Treasure* disaster was the largest oiled-bird rescue ever attempted. A huge railway warehouse at Cape Town became the cleanup center for birds from the Robben and Dassen Island breeding colonies.

Over nineteen thousand more penguins were rescued from Dassen Island before they could swim out and become oiled. Ships took them 600 miles (965 km) east before releasing them. Scientists thought the penguins would know where to go to head home, and they did. But the journey back to Dassen Island took them nearly three weeks. Meanwhile, volunteers worked hard to clean up the oiled water and beaches. They also rescued the abandoned chicks and cared for them.

It was a huge effort. For the bird-cleaning operation alone, about forty-five thousand volunteers helped 130 team leaders from International Bird Rescue. The task went on for twelve weeks and took more than three hundred 6.6-gallon (25-liter) jugs of liquid detergent in total. The volunteers eventually cleaned more than eighteen thousand oil-coated birds, most of them African penguins. The transport and release of unoiled birds from the colonies saved even more lives. Scientists believe more than 90 percent of the penguins at Robben and Dassen Island colonies survived, thanks to the rescue efforts.

In holding pens, volunteers feed oiled birds waiting to be cleaned (*above*).

Cleaned penguins could take a dip in wading pools (*right*) before being released to the ocean.

TURNING POINT

The *MV Treasure* disaster focused the world's attention on the shrinking African penguin population. If the pattern continued, scientists realized, these birds would soon disappear from the wild. Since then several operations have been racing to help the penguins.

The World Association of Zoos and Aquariums (WAZA) has tried to boost African penguin numbers in zoos and institutions, where animals can be cared for and visitors can learn about the penguins up close. By 2016, 106 zoos and aquariums around the world were housing and breeding a total of 2,796 African penguins, about 1,000 more penguins than in 2005. WAZA has also funded fieldwork at the colonies and sent volunteers to work with scientists trying to help African penguin chicks survive.

A young visitor watches African penguins at the New Jersey State Aquarium.

In 2006 scientists ran a trial effort on Dyer Island to give the penguins protected burrows, more like the guano burrows the birds once used. The goal was a higher survival rate of African penguin chicks, with nests protected from predators and the hot sun. Two hundred igloo-shaped fiberglass burrows were placed on that island's nesting site. However, these burrows proved to be heat traps. Heat stress frequently drove the adults into the ocean to cool off, and predators stole their eggs.

In later breeding seasons, at several colonies, scientists tested other artificial burrows, in various shapes and made of different materials. African penguin researcher Peter Barham reported, "The most successful in my studies on Robben Island were wooden A-frames, with cement igloos a close second." But experts are still looking for the best possible artificial burrow type for different nesting sites.

Penguin pairs quickly claimed artificial burrows such as this fiberglass one during trial runs.

In 2008 the South African government kicked off an experiment to protect the penguins' critical food source, anchovies and sardines. From 2008 through 2010, the Island Closures Task Team created "no-take" zones around Saint Croix Island and Bird Island, two African penguin nesting sites off the country's southern coast. These zones made it illegal to fish closer than 12 miles (20 km) from shore during the breeding season. Leaders hoped this would help the African penguin population rebound by ensuring parents could find enough food for their chicks.

Fatter young penguins are more likely to survive than slimmer ones, so researchers weigh chicks in the colonies to monitor their health.

However, in 2009 the International Union for Conservation of Nature (IUCN) estimated the African penguin population at just 25,262 breeding pairs. By 2010 experts found that the penguin population had shrunk even further. That year these penguins were officially listed as endangered on the international Red List of Threatened Species.

The controlled fishing experiment continued from 2011 through 2013, with the no-take zone shifted to Robben and Dassen Islands. The goal was to find out what effect the fishing restrictions had on chick rearing. Scientists learned that in most cases, the number of chicks raised didn't change from previous years. However, most chicks weighed and measured as part of the study grew faster than in past nesting seasons. Experts believe that will improve the survival rate of juvenile birds.

When the experiment ended, the debate began. Some scientists believed that the ban on fishing did boost chick survival and that it should be continued. Other scientists argued that fishing quotas (limits on how much of each kind of fish can be caught) were enough to help protect the penguins' main food source.

As the debate over how to help African penguins continued, scientists began one more experiment to try to make a difference for the endangered birds.

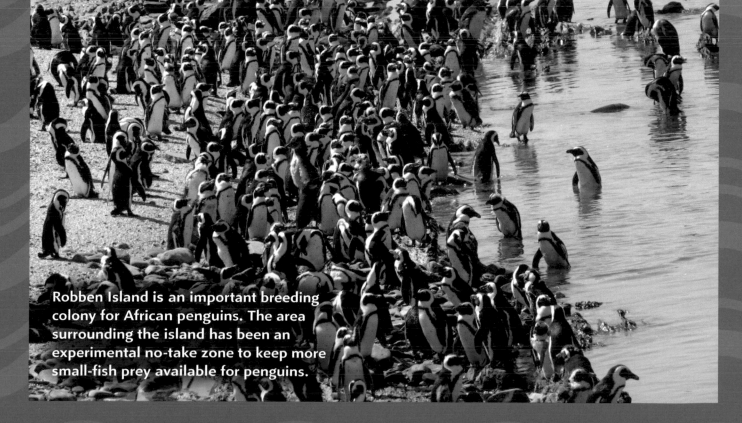

Robben Island is an important breeding colony for African penguins. The area surrounding the island has been an experimental no-take zone to keep more small-fish prey available for penguins.

RAISING THE FUTURE

In the Chick Rearing Unit, chicks are weighed to monitor their growth (*top*). Then they're fed. The fish smoothie fed to very young chicks is like the partly digested food they would get from their parents (*bottom*).

In 2011 the Southern African Foundation for the Conservation of Coastal Birds (SANCCOB) launched a Chick Rearing Unit to help African penguins. Volunteers worked with scientists to rescue abandoned chicks from the colonies and feed them while they grew. The chicks responded well to this care and grew into healthy juveniles. When those juveniles were released, they swam away into the ocean as readily as chicks raised by penguin parents.

Chick rearing continues to be an important project and a big job.

Every morning at five thirty, every chick at the Chick Rearing Unit is weighed. Then at each of the chick's six feedings that day, it receives 10 percent of its body weight in food. Chicks up to one month old receive a kind of fish smoothie. From then until they're three months old, chicks are fed this smoothie mixed with tiny bits of hand-cut sardine fillets. Three- to four-month-old chicks receive trimmed fish tails.

Feeding the juveniles is a smelly, messy job, but volunteers do it knowing they're helping save African penguins.

Finally, once chicks start replacing their downy coats with juvenile feathers, they're fed whole sardines or anchovies. Each chick is usually fed two or three 6-inch-long (15 cm) fish twice a day. And when the birds are fully fledged, strong, and healthy, they're ready for the ocean. So the juveniles are carefully transported to colony beaches—sites that researchers hope they'll one day return to, to mate and raise chicks of their own.

Stephen van der Spuy, executive director of SANCCOB, reported that the project seems to be a success. "The idea was to get as many African penguins back into the wild population as possible," he said. "And it's working!" SANCCOB has two chick-rearing sites, on the Western Cape and on the Eastern Cape. The two sites together took in about nine hundred abandoned chicks (including chicks hatched from abandoned eggs) in 2014, he said. The unit isn't able to save every rescued chick, because some have infections or have been very underfed. But an average of more than 60 percent survive to be released as juveniles.

To save even more penguins, the Chick Rearing Unit is hatching more abandoned eggs and raising the chicks that hatch.

"Collected eggs could have been laid recently or be fairly well developed," says Romy Klusener, the Chick Rearing Unit supervisor at SANCCOB. "There's only one way to tell—candling." This involves holding the egg up to a bright light to show the embryo developing inside. An expert can tell how well developed it is. And that determines how the egg will be incubated, or kept warm until the chick hatches.

Eggs that still need a lot of time for the embryo to develop are put into incubators that keep the air about 97.7°F (36.5°C) with 45 percent humidity (amount of moisture in the air). The SANCCOB team discovered that African penguin eggs needed to be turned often for the embryos to develop. So they use incubators that automatically roll the eggs little by little, completing one full turn every twenty-four hours. Once a day, human helpers also turn each egg end to end.

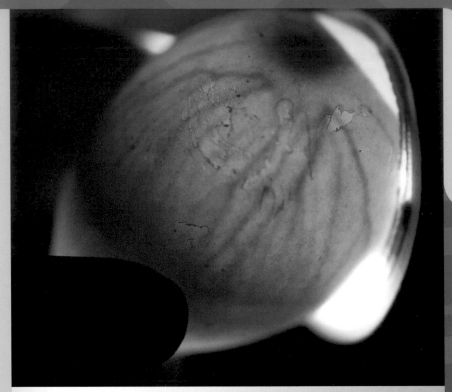

A recently laid egg is examined *(top)*. **The red lines are the part of a system that will carry nutrients (food material) from the egg yolk to the developing embryo (baby chick). In an incubator** *(bottom)*, **eggs are slowly turned to help evenly distribute both heat and nutrients inside the eggs.**

By the time a chick has been developing for about thirty-eight days, it is nearly ready to hatch. These eggs are moved to an incubator where the air is a little cooler (95°F, or 35°C) and very moist (60 percent humidity). The additional moisture softens the shell just enough to make it easier for the chick to peck its way out.

Sometimes a chick is fed drops of water as it works to hatch.

Christoph Schwitzer is one of a team of scientists looking to the future for African penguins. Schwitzer leads the Research for Conservation Program at the Bristol Conservation and Science Foundation and Bristol Zoo Gardens (a member of WAZA). "Our ultimate goal," he said, "is the translocation [shifting] of a colony to a new site—one away from people and close to a good supply of fish."

The Boulders Beach penguin colony is a tourist site that's close to homes and busy roads.

Historically, African penguins do sometimes adopt a new colony site. For example, in the 1980s, they started nesting at Boulders Beach and Stony Point on the mainland, near Cape Town. Now scientists are hoping to encourage penguins to launch a new colony at a site that's farther from busy roads and areas where people live and closer to offshore schools of sardines and anchovies. They plan to do this by using young adults that have grown up at the Chick Rearing Unit. But these experts still need to learn one key fact about African penguins before they'll try to start a new colony.

Scientists need to understand at what point young penguins adopt a colony site. Do they remain loyal to the colony where they hatched as chicks? Or the site where they first enter the ocean as juveniles?

To find out, researchers are injecting tiny, lightweight transponders (devices that transmit radio signals) just under the skin on the backs of all juveniles raised by the Chick Rearing Unit. Then, each year, about fifty birds that hatched on Robben Island are being released at the Stony Point colony site or on Robben Island. The transponder lets scientists track where the penguins later return to breed.

It can take three years or more for the adults to choose a colony where they'll return every year to raise a family.

This adult is carrying nesting material to its nest site on Dassen Island.

Not all the released birds have survived to breed. But those that did are surprising researchers. Schwitzer reported, "So far, about half returned to their hatching site. The other half went to several different colonies—ones other than either the Robben Island or Dassen Island colonies. This means the issue of site fidelity (loyalty) seems to be overrated."

That discovery has scientists excited about starting a trial colony at a brand-new site. They hope that juveniles released at that new site will return there when they're ready to breed, founding a colony where more chicks will hatch each year. And with the right protections and nearby ocean full of fish to eat, the African penguin population may finally grow stronger once again.

RESCUED!

Shivering with fear and peeping, the abandoned female chick is scooped up by a SANCCOB volunteer. She's wrapped in a warm towel and fed small pieces of fish. With her tummy full, she sleeps. When she wakes, she moans until she's lifted and fed again. One day after another passes this way. She's soon strong again. And much fatter.

The chick's downy coat is rubbed clean, and she's wrapped in something warm.

A volunteer checks the chick's weight to prepare for her day's feeding schedule.

The chick already has big webbed feet with claw-tipped toes. They're useful for walking on land, and one day soon, they'll be perfect for steering while swimming in the ocean.

In between feedings, the female chick is put into a pen with other chicks. When they peck and push her, she pecks and pushes back. When they press against her and stay still, she huddles with them and naps.

Gradually, her food changes as she grows. The female chick changes too, shedding clumps of down for feathers until she's a fully-fledged juvenile. Sometimes she's placed in a pen with a pool of water. And she wades in.

One day the juvenile female is lifted from her holding pen. But this time, she isn't fed. She's placed in a box. "*Haw! Haw! Bray!*" She complains in her adult-sounding voice.

Other penguins call too, and when she peeks through holes in the box, she spies more boxes—lots more boxes. Then there's no more chance to keep looking because she's bounced around and has to work to stay on her feet. At last, the box is still again, and a warm, salty breeze puffs through the holes.

When the box is opened and tipped, the juvenile female scrambles out. She's on sand alongside lots of other juveniles. Waves slop ashore straight ahead, and she hurries toward them. The young penguin wades into the frothy surf and, for the very first time in her life, dives into the cool ocean. Then she swims away.

She'll come ashore sometimes to rest and once a year to molt, but it will be three years before she's ready to join a breeding colony. Then she and her mate will raise a family of their own.

Thanks to the help of the SANCCOB Chick Rearing Unit, this female has a better chance to survive. And the African penguin population has a little bit better chance of surviving too.

These young are released into the sea at Stony Point, Betty's Bay. Each year, SANCCOB releases as many as nine hundred juvenile African penguins into the wild.

SAVING OTHER PENGUINS

All kinds of penguins, including Adélies that nest in Antarctica, are being affected by global climate change and are seeing their populations decline. Human efforts to help Antarctic penguins have been limited because of the difficulties of their extremely remote location. But people around the world are working to make a difference for other endangered penguins.

In New Zealand, where yellow-eyed penguins *(top)* spread out to nest alone in forested areas, their breeding sites are protected as nature reserves.

Galápagos penguins *(bottom right)* nest in colonies on Isabela and Fernandina Islands, north of the equator, where the breeding season is very warm. To help them, a team used the island's lava rock to build 120 shaded nesting sites.

Northern rockhopper penguins *(bottom left)* mainly nest on Nightingale Island in the Tristan da Cunha island group in the South Atlantic. Volunteers there are trapping rats and mice, which prey on the penguins' eggs and young chicks, to reduce the large population of predators.

Helping endangered penguins is an ongoing effort. Researchers hope that organized operations such as these will help to ensure that these penguin species survive long into the future.

Author's Note

Wildlife conservation stories always feel personal to me, and the African penguin's plight especially touched me. That's because I have personal experience with penguins. Thanks to the National Science Foundation's Antarctic Artists and Writers Program, I spent the summers of 1996 and 1998 camping out with over 160,000 Adélie penguins in Antarctica, watching them, listening to them, and caring about them. In fact, because I was working with David Ainley's research team, I had the opportunity to hold a three-month-old chick while weighing it. If the adults hadn't already won over my heart for all kinds of penguins, that did it. A downy penguin chick is still the softest, fuzziest animal I've ever touched.

Later, during the fourteen years I lived in New Zealand, I also had the opportunity to visit a yellow-eyed penguin research site, watch those birds, and learn about efforts to help their struggling population.

So when I heard about the urgent situation facing African penguins, I had to dig in, learn more, and find a hopeful ending. Learning how humans have hurt this population broke my heart. But people are working hard to rescue the chicks—even when they're still developing inside their eggs. There was the positive twist I had hoped to find! I couldn't wait to share their story, which continues to unfold each day.

African penguins will likely need many years to fully rebound to safe population numbers, and conservation efforts will need the help of lots of people who care—animal scientists, environmentalists, writers, and more. How will you find your own way to help penguin populations survive?

Did You Know?

Adult African penguins call to one another with donkey-like brays. It's why they're sometimes called jackass penguins (*jackass* is another term for donkey). They're also called black-footed penguins, even though their feet are more pink than black.

Males are usually a little larger than females and have larger beaks. Pairs are often seen preening each other's feathers. Besides helping the pair stay bonded, this removes parasites (living things that exist at a cost to other living things). It also keeps the penguin's waterproof feathers arranged in a dense coat, which shields its skin from the cold ocean water.

African penguins can dive as deep as 200 feet (61 meters) and stay underwater for more than five minutes.

What looks pink above the penguin's eyes is a special body part that keeps it from overheating. As the penguin's body warms up, blood flow increases to that area. The lack of feathers over that area lets heat radiate away as the blood flows through it. That cools the penguin.

Timeline

Note: Population numbers reported are estimates, and reports from different experts and organizations vary.

1800s The African penguin population is estimated to be about four million adult penguins.

Mid-1800s People begin scraping guano from nesting sites in South Africa.

1900–1930s Penguin eggs are harvested annually for humans to eat.

1956–1957 The International Union for the Conservation of Nature (IUCN) estimates the number of African penguins to be 141,000 breeding pairs.

1967 The South African government bans the harvesting of penguin eggs.

1979–1980 The IUCN estimates the number of African penguins has fallen to about 69,000 breeding pairs.

1991 Guano scraping from penguin nesting sites is outlawed in South Africa, although it had stopped earlier.

2000 In June the ore carrier *MV Treasure* sinks, spilling fuel oil near several large African penguin breeding colonies. A huge rescue effort is launched.

2004 Scientists determine that the shift of the Benguela upwelling away from penguin colonies is linked to climate change.

2006–2007 The IUCN estimates that the African penguin population is about 36,000 breeding pairs.

2008–2013 The South African government's Island Closures Task Team sets a 12-mile (20 km) "no-take" zone restricting fishing around key African penguin colonies (2008–2010, Saint Croix and Bird Islands; 2011–2013, Robben and Dassen Islands).

2010 The African penguin is listed as endangered on the IUCN's Red List of Threatened Species after the 2009 estimate drops to 25,262 breeding pairs. Conservation experts and South African government officials hold a conference to create an emergency action plan.

2011 SANCCOB officially launches the Chick Rearing Unit to save abandoned African penguin chicks (although conservation volunteers have worked to rescue abandoned chicks since 2006).

2013 The South African minister of water and environmental affairs, B. E. E. (Edna) Molewa, signs an emergency action plan for helping the African penguin population.

2014 BirdLife South Africa reports there are about 19,000 breeding pairs of African penguins left in South Africa and about 5,000 pairs in Namibia.

2015 The World Association of Zoos and Aquariums (WAZA) continues housing and breeding a total of 2,796 African penguins at 106 zoos and aquariums around the world, about 1,000 more penguins than in 2005.

2016 Scientists continue to track released juveniles and work toward a plan for shifting a colony.

What is one thing you would like to be able to add to this timeline in the future?

Source Notes

27 Peter Barham, telephone interview with author, July 24, 2015.

31 Stephen van der Spuy, telephone interview with author, July 31, 2015.

32 Romy Klusener, telephone interview with author, August 17, 2015.

34 Christoph Schwitzer, telephone interview with author, July 21, 2015.

37 Ibid.

Glossary

burrow: a hole or tunnel an animal lives in

colony: a group of the same kind of animals living together or gathered to mate and raise young

embryo: an animal in the early stages of development, as it forms basic tissues and organs

guano: waste droppings from African penguins or other seabirds

habitat: the natural home environment of a plant or animal

humidity: the amount of moisture in the air

incubate: to cover and keep an egg warm for the young animal inside to develop

molt: to shed old feathers and replace them with new feathers

nutrient: a substance that provides protein, vitamins, and minerals essential for growth

parasite: a living thing that lives in or on another living thing, often harming the host

predator: an animal that hunts and eats other living things in order to live

preen: to groom feathers by straightening and cleaning with the beak

Find Out More

Check out these books and websites to discover even more:

African Penguin Chicks Rescued as Fish Stocks Are Depleted—YouTube
https://www.youtube.com/watch?v=IacbojIVKik
Watch a news clip from the South African Broadcasting Corporation that shows the SANCCOB chick-rearing operation up close during the busy chick season, in May 2016.

African Penguin Facts for Kids: Penguins, Boulders Beach
http://www.kids-world-travel-guide.com/african-penguin.html
This web page features photos and facts about African penguins, giving visitors a glimpse into life at Boulders Beach penguin colony.

African Penguins at Boulders Beach, Cape Town
https://www.youtube.com/watch?v=kqNeUmTry9Q
Take a virtual trip to this African penguin colony to watch and listen to these birds.

Arlon, Penelope. *Penguins*. New York: Scholastic, 2012.
Investigate all seventeen different kinds of penguins. Find out how African penguins are similar to the others and what sets other types of penguins apart.

Conley, Kate A. *South Africa*. Mankato, MN: Child's World, 2016.
Explore the geography and culture of the country that's home to African penguins.

"They're Not Revolting—They're Molting!": Adventure Insider
https://adventureaquarium.wordpress.com/2013/09/26/theyre-not-revolting-theyre-molting/
Penguins in zoos and aquariums molt too! Follow African penguins step by step through the molting process at Adventure Aquarium in New Jersey.

Waxman, Laura Hamilton. *Emperor Penguins: Antarctic Diving Birds*. Minneapolis: Lerner Publications, 2016.
What traits help emperor penguins to survive in their extreme environment in Antarctica? Learn about these penguins by comparing them with other birds.

Index

Photo Acknowledgments

The images in this book are used with the permission of: © Richard Du Toit/Minden Pictures, p. 1; © iStockphoto.com/ IADA (fish throughout); © Arco Images GmbH/Alamy, p. 4; © robertharding/Alamy, p. 5; © Mike Korostelev www. mkorostelev.com/Moment/Getty Images, p. 6; © Martin Harvey/Gallo Images/Getty Images, p. 7; © Cormac McCreesh/ Gallo Images/Getty Images, p. 8; © imageBROKER/Alamy, p. 9; © Laura Westlund/Independent Picture Service, pp. 10, 20; © Martin Harvey/Gallo Images/Getty Images, p. 11; © Jason Edwards/National Geographic/Getty Images, p. 12; © Hoberman Collection/UIG/Getty Images, p. 13; © Homebrew Films Company/Gallo Images/Getty Images, p. 14; © Michael Langford/gallo Images/Getty Images, p. 15; © Jeff Rotman/Minden Pictures, pp. 16–17; © Meriel Lland/ Photolibrary/Getty Images, p. 18; © Jurgen and Christine Sohns/Minden Pictures, p. 19; © Chris & Monique Fallows/ naturepl.com, pp. 20–21; © TOM WALMSLEY/NPL/Minden Pictures, p. 22; AP Photo/John Hrusa, p. 23; © epa european pressphoto agency b.v./Alamy, p. 24 (all); © Martin Harvey/Photolibrary/Getty Images, p. 25 (left); AP Photo/Obed Zilwa, p. 25 (right); AP Photo/Daniel Hulshizer, p. 26; © Chris and Tilde Stuart/Minden Pictures, p. 27; © ZUMA Press, Inc. Alamy, p. 29; © Cheryl-Samantha Owen/naturepl.com, pp. 30 (all), 32 (all), 33; © RODGER BOSCH/AFP/Getty Images, p. 31; © Colin Marshall/Minden Pictures, pp. 34–35; © Thierry Falise/LightRocket/Getty Images, p. 36; © Martin Harvey/ Getty Images, p. 37; © JENNIFER BRUCE/AFP/Getty Images, p. 38 (top); © Barbara Haddock Taylor/Baltimore Sun/MCT/ Getty Images, p. 38 (bottom); © epa european pressphoto agency b.v./Alamy, p. 39; © RODGER BOSCH/AFP/Getty Images, pp. 40–41; © Art Wolfe/Getty Images, p. 42 (top); © Roger Horrocks/Getty Images, p. 42 (bottom left); © Joel Sartore/agency/Getty Images, p. 42 (bottom right); © Martin Harvey/Photolibrary RM/Getty Images, p. 44.

Front cover: © Peter Chadwick/Gallo Images/Getty Images; © iStockphoto.com/IADA (fish).

Back cover: © Claudia Paulussen/REX/Shutterstock.